THE DAY OF THE DEAD

by Bob Barner

translated by Teresa Mlawer

EL DÍA DE LOS MUERTOS

Holiday House / New York

HOLIDAY HOUSE is registered in the U.S. Patent and Trademark Office.

Printed and Bound in April 2010 at Kwong Fat Offset Printing Co., Ltd.,

Dongguan City, Guang Dong Province, China.

The text typeface is Eatwell Tall.

The artwork was created with cut, torn, and crumpled papers covered with pastel dust, pencil, and printing inks.

www.holidayhouse.com

First Edition

1 3 5 7 9 10 8 6 4 2

Library of Congress Cataloging-in-Publication Data

Barner, Bob.

The Day of the Dead = El Día de los Muertos / by Bob Barner ; translated by Teresa Mlawer. — 1st ed.

p. cm.

English and Spanish.

ISBN 978-0-8234-2214-2 (hardcover)

1. All Souls' Day—Mexico—Juvenile literature. I. Title. II. Title: Día de los Muertos.

GT4995.A4B37 2010

394.264—dc22

2009049721

For my inspiring friend Dilys and
the inspired artist José Guadalupe Posada

We celebrate our ancestors on the Day of the Dead

El Día de los Muertos honramos a los antepasados

with offerings of flowers, sugar skulls, and bread.

con ofrendas de flores, calaveras
de azúcar, y pan horneado.

We make tacos, empanadas, mole, and treats.

Hacemos tacos, empanadas, mole, y platos deliciosos.

Smell incense that burns smoky and sweet.

Quemamos incienso con ese olor maravilloso.

Before we go out, everything must be done.

Hay que tener todo listo antes de la partida

Pack up our bundles before the setting sun.

y empacar bien las cosas mientras hay luz del día.

Under twinkling stars and the moon glowing bright,
Bajo estrellas que brillan y una luna muy clara,

light the candles that flicker with soft yellow light.

encendemos las velas amarillas y blancas.

Mark a path for the spirits
with the petals of flowers.

El camino a los espíritus indicamos
con pétalos de flores que cortamos.

We dance, sing,

bailamos y cantamos,

and remember
the loved ones for hours.

y durante varias horas
a nuestros seres queridos recordamos.

Celebrate our ancestors
on the Day of the Dead.

Honremos a los antepasados
en el Día de los Muertos.

We smell the sweet flowers
as we lie down for bed.

Y cuando a dormir nos retiramos,
el dulce olor de las flores aspiramos.

About el Día de los Muertos

Millions of people from Mexico and parts of Central and South America observe one of Latin America's most popular holidays called el Día de los Muertos in Spanish and the Day of the Dead in English. It is a special time for remembering loved ones who are no longer living and is celebrated every year from October 31 until November 2.

People prepare for the holiday by baking or buying special foods. *Pan de muertos*, or bread of the dead, is a sweet bread baked only for this special holiday. It has a tiny skeleton doll baked inside. The person lucky enough to get the little skeleton in his or her piece of bread can make a wish that will come true. Sugar skulls, or *calaveras de azúcar*, come  decorated in bright colors. They can be eaten at the end of the celebration. People also gather the favorite foods of their deceased loved ones. Tamales are a popular treat at the celebrations. They are cornmeal cakes filled with meat, wrapped in a cornhusk, and steamed before eating.

Altars for the departed, decorated with *cempazuchitl*, or marigolds, and candles, are displayed in homes and schools. Sweet-smelling incense is burned to attract the spirits of the departed.

On the night of November 2, families go to the cemetery. They spread the petals of marigold flowers, burn incense, and light candles to welcome the spirits to the celebration. Then they dance, sing, have a picnic, and share memories of their loved ones. Families leave the flowers on the graves at the end of the celebration as they begin their journey home.

The popular Mexican artist José Guadalupe Posada (1852-1913) inspired some of the skeleton characters in this book. His engravings of skeletons and the skeleton lady with a large flowered hat, *La Catrina*, have become symbols of the Day of the Dead holiday.